Gold is everywhere, inside and
One only has to open one's ey
To find gold, one must first bt

Globlquest Publishing
globalquest28@gmail.com

© Keith Simons 2021
www.spiritual-narratives.net

National Library of Australia
Cataloguing-in-Publication data:

Simons, Keith, 1949-,
Parrelsitus/Keith Simons.
ISBN 978-0-9758365-3-8
1. Simons, Keith, 1949-.

Cover artwork
Philosopher in Meditation by Rembrandt

Foreword

The book in your hands is a continuation of previous books and their accompanying inner processes. Those 'processes' warrant a book in themselves, but at least a general outline here will help to provide a larger context for 'Parelsitus: Thirty Pieces of Gold'.

A linear progression can be outlined by way of mentioning my previous books, Portal: Awakening to Being (2012), Elucia (2016) and Poetica Esoterica (2018). Portal was the outcome of a tumultuous phase of my life: when my younger son suffered a 'breakdown'. That led me to a Native American psychiatrist and healer, Lewis Mehl-Madrona, and his colleges, Rocky and Barbara. Via these three I was 'initiated' into an Indigenous 'deep talking and listening' (Hocokah in Lakota) practice. This was life-changing in ways that I couldn't have imagined at that time. It led to an inter-dimensional group dynamic that in turn led to the book Portal.

A few years later, I was guided to study a nine- volume series of translated lectures by Rudolf Steiner. The message received was that I needed to read through these lectures (Karmic Relationships) before writing my next book. Indeed, on finishing the Steiner lectures, a room became available that was to be my study for the months ahead. I furnished the room to my liking and then began transcribing, section by section, that which flowed through me from the discarnate dimension. I intuitively knew it was Steiner who was communicating through me, but I also knew that Rudolf Steiner was no more: but rather a soul that had incarnated many times, with many names. I asked for a name to be used for the soul who had been Rudolf Steiner in the previous embodiment. The name 'Elucia' flashed into consciousness. Elucia meaning 'being of light'. Hence, the book 'Elucia' emerged.

Following this, our (my wife, Leanne, and I) lives took on a different outer direction. Parelsitus was a further inter-dimensional encounter with another soul. All such souls are what Elucia refers to as belonging to 'soul-clusters', that in Buddhism is known as 'Sanga'; a spiritually engaged community. Therefore, when Elucia is mentioned in Parelsitus, the reader may have a brief context to relate to. Reading Portal and Elucia would also provide a wider 'soul cluster' context to Parelsitus, however Parelsitus can also be read as a stand-alone book, as it is the transmission of a particular soul with its own signficance and cadence.

Contents

Introduction

Introduction

This is a courageous experiment the author is undertaking: moving from one discarnate soul to another, with the opportunity for further biographies from within our inter-dimensional soul-group in the future, God willing.

My own biography is different from Elucia's and the author's, yet intimately interwoven with both. My language will be somewhat at variance with others, as should be. We are all developing our own syntheses of universal archetypes and particular modes of expression. My orientation is deeply personal and interpersonal and spans across many related fields of inquiry and ongoing research. The tensions between polarities and the experience of creative paradox is especially relevant to my focus, but as a discarnate soul they take on inter-dimensional lateral (non-linear) significance.

May this collaboration bear ripe fruit!

Part 1

INTENTION

Thy Will be Done

1   Will

The soul qualities that have interested me for many incarnations, and within trans-earthly realms, are those that strengthen the being and develop capacity for integration and wholeness. This is the potential of all beings who have mentally reflective capacities.

Of these qualities it the 'will' that I want to focus on. What do we mean by will? Imagining an action is not the same as doing it. Even where I am now, the will is operative. I cannot exercise my will through a body, but my will is active in communicating with the author.

Will is the movement from internal choice to outer action. When the will chooses a certain action, the field of multiple possibilities collapses into a manifested reality. The other possibilities are sacrificed for the time being.

Where I am, the choice does not manifest directly in a material or physical way, but influences the incarnate realm through the intercommunication with an incarnated being. The will is the force that moves in a particular direction motivated by choice. This quality is of tremendous importance to your world at this time. Wilfulness allows souls to act, and the sense of impotency and limitation must give way for the will to exercise its power. Therefore, consciousness of choice and wilfulness become gateways to transformation.

Spiritual attainment is not possible without wise choices and active willpower. My incarnational achievements were not random fly-by-nights. They were substantial steps along paths of personal development, with goals shared by energies of universal wisdom, creativity and joy. When my personal will is conjoined to the greater will of godlike beings, marvellous evolutional progress is achieved. This merger of different cosmic levels of energies furthers the destiny of earthly evolution. The outcome is tempered and influenced by degrees of freedom. As you may now be aware, my transmissions will have a more psychological and analytical quality than Elucia's. That too is my choice and motivation. That too is an exercise of my will to action.

Let us journey into exciting depths of insight and empowerment, tempered by sensible choices and enhanced willpower, to act wisely and effectively wherever we are.

2   Dedication

'Dedication' is a word that scares many people, but without a degree of dedication, the will flutters about like a leaf blown in the wind. However a weak will is not the only challenge, for an undisciplined will can be powerful, but seldom in ways that bring consistent peace and creative joy.

Dedication implies developing the capacity to discern, choose and act in a focused way. Discernment allows for awareness of different possibilities and their qualitative contrasts. Wise discernment develops from experience, and is the capacity to inwardly know what is a better choice and what is not. Discerning choices can reveal the mark of a mature soul. Actions that are a consequence of such choices tend to prove their value. If discernment is directed towards an altruistic vision and motivated by a joyful sense of meaningful action, dedication can naturally follow.

Dedication is a sign that you have discovered an aspect of your soul's mission and it then expresses as a love of work in action. This in turn becomes a powerful determining factor in shaping ones' living energies in service to the universal goal of evolutional creativity and harmony. Dedication coupled with will is a potent agent of transformational change.

In your age of plenty, a major obstacle to dedicated will is the force of distraction. Therefore, a practice of discipline is vital. This I developed in my previous incarnation by balancing creative solitude with worldly engagement.

As an embodied soul, you cannot live out every inner gift and possible manifestation. But you can choose something you feel naturally drawn to, and dedicate yourself to exploring and refining it, allowing for changes of direction in its unfolding.

Meditate, therefore, on the themes of will and dedication.

3   Incarnations

Souls who have developed strong psychological and spiritual qualities will have had at least one or two noteworthy previous incarnations and are likely to have influenced the progress of earthly culture. There is an obvious principle at play here. Soul qualities have an evolutional nature that seek favourable circumstances for rebirth.

In the past 2,600 years I have had three especially influential incarnations, and others that were important in lesser ways. In the fifth century BC I was a significant figure in Greece. Even then, I'd cultivated many good soul qualities from earlier incarnations, but this rebirth had a distinctly 'modern' feel about it. In fact, I was the first to bring into the public arena many philosophical and psychological dialectics that were strongly influenced by Pythagoreans. I, in turn, had a strong influence on Elucia some hundreds of years later, and indirectly on Keith, the present biographer, and his partner.

My turn of mind was especially able to sit in the midst of paradox and reconcile opposites. This took on curious and inventive expressions that have been a font of scholarly debate ever since. The primary foundation of this flexible mental capacity was my experiential understanding of the *one* behind the *many*. It has been suggested that I should be known as a Monist and opponent to the Dualists of that time. Expressing this paradoxical unity was creatively challenging, but also exhilarating, and poetry became my main style of literary output.

I then had a number of lesser incarnations of both genders where I developed specific qualities, until in the seventeenth century I incarnated in a favourable manner to integrate many of those threads. Into this I brought my pre-Socratic impulse to greater fruition and became an influential part of Renaissance Europe. This incarnation offered favourable circumstances to bring many complementary arts and sciences to a ripeness that were advanced even for those times. I passionately sought to blend the mundane with the esoteric and to show how the deeper laws of one govern the other. Alchemy, astrology and medicine were my prime areas of study and practice. A legacy was left behind that others picked up on and advanced, including myself, in the third of my incarnations externally renowned by historians. Not that I disparage the significance of such incarnations, but they are the ones recorded for posterity, whilst others are as if they never occurred. The other incarnations were merely in circumstances that went unrecorded in your history books, but Life has its own library and the chapters of evolutional development are imprinted and archived where it most matters.

The third distinguished incarnation was not so long ago. Many of the previous areas of deep interest were picked up again and further developed within a twentieth-century setting and cultural milieu. I was now more interested in discovering new ways for knowledge: esoteric, scientific, artistic and the rather new discipline of depth psychology to complement them, becoming, as it were, a coherent multi-disciplinary movement of inner health, balance and sanity. In this, as with all souls, I succeeded in varying degrees.

The complementary part of my biography will follow. What have I been doing between incarnations, including now, within the transcarnate realms?

4 Transcarnations

There are major features of transcarnational growth that are especially possible in this intermediate space rather than when embodied. A key feature is what can be called 'renunciation'. It is understood that attachments to physical and sensory objects of desire tend to inhibit deeper inner psychological and spiritual growth. Holding onto such attachments in transcarnate realms is what your metaphoric language refers to as 'hell'. Renunciation is therefore the capacity to sacrifice and let go of psychic attachments that have accumulated during incarnations.

The degree to which this is a challenge largely depends on how attached one was, especially during the previous incarnation, and even more so in the latter part of that physical life span. As I was able to renounce attachments, the spaciousness of consciousness expanded and my capacity to join with other souls in meaningful cluster-oriented work became enhanced.

Another feature of transcarnational growth is becoming more focused on the greater evolutionary mission. Various skills and refined capacities developed both incarnationally and transcarnationally are perceived in the larger context of this mission. In this sense, one's mission is an archetype, a guiding force. Ultimately all individuated souls' missions, belonging to the same general universalised mission, are serving the same overarching vision and evolutional imperative, meaning that future cosmic goals must eventually be reached. The illusion within freedom is that individuated goals not aligned with cosmic law can equally compete with this cosmic mission. A soul's mission belongs eventually to a coherent and complementary alignment with cosmic intelligence and purpose. I have been refining such a cosmic perception, and this is opening new doors of possibility for future incarnational service.

One more transcarnational aspect of growth will suffice. What might be termed 'faith' for you, as incarnated souls, is direct experience for me here. The capacity to directly experience without limitations of space and time permits for growth in eternal timelessness. This quality for you is possible through transcendentalism, but here it is the norm. It can be brought into future incarnations as a natural orientation towards meditative and other spiritual practices. I have been developing this capacity as a conscious part of my mission during many of my intermediate transcarnational lives. Yet the transcarnational phases between incarnations are even more acutely experienced as 'lives' than when incarnated. They are vividly expansive and beautiful in ways that are indescribable in human language.

Nonetheless, you who are incarnated have the opportunity to transfer these greater spiritual and psychological attributes into your evolving world, and this is a major part of the greater cosmic vision and mission.

Part 2

TRANSFERENCE

Embrace the largesse of your soul

5 Technology

The extreme mix of elements now existing in your earthly realm has created challenges for many souls that are presenting in unique ways. The essentially bipolar nature of this mix leads to myriads of dysfunctional manifestations, both collectively and individually.

It needs to be understood that technology is a powerful extension of materialism. Not something different, but rather an outcome of human identification with externalities.

Technology removes the soul even further from the spiritual nature of real earthly existence. It is not evil in itself but can usurp the focus on living elements and replace them with dead, inorganic matter. This is what Elucia pointed to as an evolving sub-species called 'Homo-Biotech'.

When such beings discarnate they enter into a strange sub-realm of souls who no longer experience a strong connection to living beings or the natural earth realm. If they desire to reincarnate it is motivated by a need to enhance their identification with technology.

What makes this a strong force, even transcarnationally, is the fact that technological experience is largely disembodied. This is not a moral issue, but a choice in evolutional direction, with consequences that cannot be understood in terms of our universe alone. Even such souls are a part of the whole.

Technology is an evolutional extension. Ultimately it is a matter of integrating it into the entire matrix, spiritualising it. Bringing all the children home to play in the garden of peace. Such children would not be obsessed with technology.

In a future world, technology will be understood as a substitute for direct experience. What need for computers when direct telepathic communication is possible?

6 Mysterium

Alchemy, Tantra and Yoga are three subjects among many that are grossly misunderstood in your materialistic, atheistic and scientific earth realm. Materialism, secularism and science are not obstacles in themselves, only when they refute that which cannot be measured with earthbound instruments.

Psychic and spiritual charlatanism hasn't helped either, but the gulf existing between authentic inter-dimensional experience and narrow beliefs, even if popular, is one of the root causes of your planetary crisis. This crisis is far greater than one of differing beliefs and ideologies. Therefore the community of true spiritual pioneers and those who support them transcend a type of modern flat-earth theology.

Alchemy, Tantra and Yoga have two main levels of operation, one of which occurs in transcarnate realms. The level that only concerns incarnate souls is an approximate replication of the level that we share with you. Keith must combine both levels to convey my meaning, because your written and spoken language is unique to your physical realm.

Alchemy is the Western equivalent of Tantra and Yoga that are essentially Eastern. They all deal with transformation, transcendence and transmutation.

My passion and mission is more to do with the psychology of mysticism, as it might be expressed in your realm. Alchemy attempted to replicate in the laboratory what really belongs to inter-dimensionality. Where I am, there are no physical laboratories. Alchemy here is immediate. It is the power of creating reality omnipresently by intention. Everything can be changed in an instant, but it is only changed into that which one chooses by way of intentionality.

When incarnated, a soul enters into a time-space realm where immediate change is generally thwarted by due process. In other words, other laws dominate, but here a most important caveat exists. The gulf between the two levels can be narrowed, and this is the true significance of these so-called mystical and occult arts. They are both ultra-sciences and arts. Alchemy, Tantra and Yoga correctly understood and applied is the process of integrating the two levels: physical and metaphysical.

The psychology surrounding this is especially concerned with the spectrum of mental phenomena that aid or obstruct this integration. Humans generally don't realise how powerful thoughts and intentions are in shaping their realities. Beliefs create blockages and open consciousness invites insights. Multi-dimensional existence is complex, and incarnational embodiment is not only complex but also caught in bubbles of illusory beliefs. The mass illusions so prevalent in your biosphere do serve to improve and refine the attempts to better articulate and convey knowledge that is needed.

Alchemy, Tantra and Yoga need to step beyond the glamorous and superficial modes in which they are being taught and become integrated with the profound ancient teachings that are still alive and well.

There is also a need for psychology to ask the right questions. The mind is a mysterium that transcends all scientific understanding. The belief that mind is some outgrowth of the brain is absurd and demonically dangerous. The best way to develop a real psychology of the mind is to recognise that you do not know what the mind is. Psyche is a mysterious God.

Not knowing creates inner space. This is a vital first step. It is where a major breakthrough must occur. The belief that you know what the mind is must be challenged and a paradox invited. For what is it that knows it doesn't know?

7 Metaphoric Psychology

Great truths can only really be expressed in human language by metaphoric psychology. In other words, by symbolic pictorial language that points towards and approximates the truth. Such pictures and stories are of vital importance to humanity and that is why art can be so spiritually significant.

An example of metaphoric psychology of tremendous importance is: *Humans are a blend of demi-God and Satan and yet capable of rising beyond this dualism to Olympian heights of unity and harmony.* This Faustian theme contains essential psychological axioms. It is clear to honest observation that humans are capable of the best and the worst that is imaginable.

Humanity, collectively and as individuals, stand between two primal forces (or temptations) and orientations. Behind this dualism there is a super-human (or to avoid the Nietzschian sense, supra-human) dimension that is a type of unified over-mind. This use of language is hugely significant for developing deep insights into human psychology and the evolution of consciousness. Metaphors like the one presented here are weighty with potential insights, epiphanies and theophanies. What makes a human being a blend of demi-God and Satan? How are we to understand this?

Psychology posits that the psyche is at the core of human experience. In a way this is true, but only if psyche is expanded to mean trans-dimensional, then the word 'consciousness' is more appropriate. Certainly psyche as related only to human beings has the more limited sense of including brain and mind together. Humans think in ways that include sensory and physiological influences with their colorations in thoughts and language. On that level a dualism between forces and orientations makes perfect sense. But if psyche is expanded to mean spiritual consciousness then such dualism can be transcended.

It is this possibility that all your world's greatest metaphors and myths point to. This use of metaphor allows psychology to mature beyond superficial analysis. It can then begin to penetrate into treasure troves and halls of Akashic wisdom. My future incarnational task will be to dedicate my will towards introducing and developing a new type of psychology that I am naming Metaphoric/Metaphorical Psychology. This book will hopefully help me remember. This will be a significant further development from my past three incarnations. Humanity is like an infant locked in a playroom with little or no idea about the larger world outside. It is now the task of our soul-cluster to open the doors of the playroom and entice the children to step outside. What a world awaits them!

8 Psychology of Identification

Can we get inside the mind of God? Is there a spiritual gene, so to speak, contained in God's creation? These are metaphorical psychological questions. If there is an affirmative response then you can know. This is the implied meaning of Gnosis, that means 'to know' in its most essential sense.

Keith worked on these questions in a memorable incarnation a few hundred years ago and I was there too as a most interested friend. These metaphorical questions concerned both of us even if the manners in which we pursued them differed. His response took on a decidedly more artistic mode of expression than mine. He used metaphor to potent advantage. His incarnational biography should be included in this series.

What is illuminating though is how we weave in and out with those souls who belong to our soul cluster. This is no closed grouping, but interpenetrates with other clusters that have affinities with our own, and we often move between various clusters in order to grow as evolutional beings. Clusters in this sense can be envisaged as fractals. Their essential motivating shapes are replications of each other. Only their more externalised formations begin to appear differently constituted. Incarnational experience identifies with these outermost variations and therefore believes in separateness. This belief is partially accurate, but only within the realm of matter and not to any profound degree. This phenomenon belongs to the psychology of identification.

Human processes of identification are complex, but have some key principles that can be easily understood. A baby identifies, to begin with, non-linguistically. Then it starts to learn naturally to name things, through imitation. Then naming develops into more sophisticated modes of language, beliefs and perceptions. The psychology of identification is therefore intrinsically entangled with language. I cannot transmit to Keith without using his vocabulary and the English language. There are interpenetrating levels of energy and communication, but these words you are reading or hearing are condensed approximations of my transmissions. These biographies are therefore truly collaborations. From our perspective they are impersonal.

We are clustered beings, and the sense of individuality belongs to your physical realm. That is not a negative, far from it. You can individuate the universal in the most powerful way, but that is also where the greatest risks belong. You cannot have the glory without the tremendous task of overcoming obstacles naturally associated with human incarnation.

You can widen and deepen your experience of identification. Then you will begin to feel, think and act more like a demi-God. But you will have to learn to dialogue with and love Satan too. Then the great reconciliation can happen, where desire and power can be as servants of the Divine.

Part 3

TRANSITION

Bridge builders you may be, and bridge-crossers your destiny

9 Parting of the Ways

Your so-called science of Psychiatry, your mainstream psychiatric institutions, academic learning facilities and private practitioners are caught in complex webs of confused ideas that largely imitate science and professional standards. There are of course individuals in the field who act with integrity and compassion and even some who have deep insight into the psyche, but the majority who operate within mainstream frameworks are unfortunately corrupted and misguided. At best their understanding is severely limited.

Psychiatry as a recognised profession has its roots in Shamanism. In the west Shamanism became narrowed into ideas about soul possession and malevolent spirits, or the Devil. In the scientific revolution that took hold in the mid-eighteenth century such beliefs were viewed as primitive superstitions. This was the age of reason, and madness was viewed as abnormalities of the brain and mind.

Trauma as the cause of mental disturbances became an increasingly popular idea and Sigmund Freud especially popularised this view with various psychoanalytic methods attempting to heal such disturbed minds. Carl Jung also acknowledged that trauma played a huge role in mental and emotional disturbances. The divergence between them became symbolic of two very different orientations that still have major divergent developments in your present time. I want to delve deeply into this divergence because it represents the two core antithetical directions psychology and psychiatry are moving in and the consequences belonging to these two streams. This is a story of the parting of the ways. We must find ways of reconciling these two streams and that will be a major focus of my next incarnation.

10 Discarnate Choices

The great successes of modern capitalism and industrialisation have introduced forms of commercial psychology with profit as their primary motivation and aim. Economics has developed alongside these movements of commerce and industry and likewise been usurped by a focus on growth and profit that has been underwritten, so to speak, by a movement of scientific rationalism and materialism. The effect this has had on generations of human populations is massive. How have spiritually sensitive and evolved individuals dealt with incarnating into an increasingly scientific, industrialised, mechanised and technological global society?

Many souls have chosen not to reincarnate into these increasingly toxic circumstances. Some souls choose to work transcarnationally and a few of those inter-dimensionally with receptive incarnated souls. This biography is an example of such inter-dimensional collaboration. The difficulty with this type of work is that in the present scientific and materialistic-dominated world you inhabit, any exposure of inter-dimensional communication, commonly described as 'channelling' will be ridiculed and dismissed. Then it becomes something close to preaching to the converted.

A greater breakthrough can only happen when individuals seriously question their own rigid beliefs and open the doors of uncertainty without going crazy in the process. This would be especially effective if couched in ways that provide a transition process. Philosophy and depth psychology can assist as they have always attempted to do. Metaphorical psychology would need to cultivate a language that speaks to the deepest qualities of sane self-observation and insight into nature in all its expressions. Of most importance is the value of the teachings, messages and invitations to explore your own potential, and in the context of evolutional unfoldment, the value to souls in future times who can take up this work and develop it further.

Discarnate souls are either metamorphosing back towards another earthly reincarnation and therefore not strongly focusing, or available to engage in inter-dimensional collaborations such as this. Some are choosing to work discarnately, although this can change whenever a choice is made to develop towards reincarnation, or they are choosing a number of other options that discarnate souls can make. Finally there are discarnate souls who are incapable of making any choices except at the most insignificant level, although even such souls are progressing within the totality.

11 Neutrality

One of the most powerful words in your English vocabulary is 'neutral'. There are other similar words that have slightly different nuances that are also powerful, such as clear, emptiness, being and consciousness. They all point towards a principle or archetype that experientially help to balance creativity and action with transcendental rest. The evolutional processes that seek to optimise human potential are similar to a seesaw or a pendulum that swings between two opposite poles. In this metaphorical context 'neutral' is the midpoint, but it also points to a transcendent dimension that can simultaneously exist with a seesaw in motion. The hub of a wheel is unmoving even as the wheel is turning. The eye of a cyclone is still even within the midst of a tremendous active force. Consciousness can be calm and empty even though physical and mental actions are being performed.

There is no identity in neutral. To fully surrender to neutral for a timeless time is to enter Samadhi or emptiness of consciousness. This can be a spiritual practice but should not be confused with existential apathy or meaninglessness.

Metaphoric psychology will penetrate into neutral as an understanding of a trinity. Taoism expresses this simply as the apex of a sacred triangle known as Tao and the two points of the triangle's base, known as Yin and Yang. The singular point at the apex is at a higher level of unified consciousness than the dualism below, and yet together they exist as a trinity.

This geometrical metaphor is somewhat more pertinent to fourth and fifth dimensional consciousness than the yin-yang circle commonly used in Taoism, that expresses the interplay of polar opposite forces but doesn't so clearly visualise the trinity. A more dynamic visualisation of this trinity can be realised by imagining the interplay down below between active and passive, moving one way and now the other, and then suddenly moving up towards the apex whereby consciousness and energy transcends movement altogether and comes to rest in neutral. At some point energy and consciousness moves down, where re-energised by neutral, it again partakes in the dynamic movement between Yin and Yang.

In this metaphorical picture Yin doesn't represent pure rest and inactivity. As in the common symbol of Taoism, there is yin within yang, and yang within yin, therefore representing some type of constant movement. It only relatively becomes more active or more passive.

Spiritual practices that are effective raise consciousness to neutral. There are many ways to do this. Meditation itself has multiple potential external expressions.

During my previous incarnation I would often experience neutrality as an adult by playing with stone and clay. Neutrality can be metaphorically depicted as mature adult consciousness temporarily becoming child like. Meditating on a clear blue day-time or night-time sky can shift consciousness too. The goal that a trinity symbolises is to integrate still, unified consciousness with the dimension of movement. This is unity within diversity, the sacred marriage of Alchemy and Tantra, Metaphorical Psychology and experiential gnosis.

12 Alchemy

Alchemy is as I have mentioned a western orientation of Tantra and Yoga. Incarnationally I researched and experienced both eastern and western modes of this art and science of transformation and transmutation of energy. Transmutation is a strange word and differs in meaning to other 'trans' words. It includes biological and chemical levels of human beingness. Therefore it is only a term relevant to an incarnated soul. My work over a number of incarnations covered all the differing modules of alchemy.

In order to focus on Alchemy, it is the western modes that are especially pertinent. Alchemy though, like Tantra, has been victim to gross misunderstandings. Even in the European Middle Ages, many misunderstood it as a type of magic or witchcraft. Then as the industrial age emerged, misunderstandings shifted their form and Alchemy was viewed more as a superstitious obsession with changes in metallurgical processes, especially that of the transmutation of base metals into gold. I was intrigued at times with this possibility but understood it as a metaphor for the spiritual and psychological transformations that Alchemy was really concerned with. I had read books such as 'The Emerald Tablet' and indeed had a part in its formation, as had some of my soul cluster within Hermeticism and Hermeneutics. Hermeneutics is the study of a science of changing elements, how elements can change into and influence each other.

Psychologically, Alchemy is concerned with the transformation of consciousness and thought. It is the portal into inter-dimensional experience and the grasping of essential principles that can be applied consistently as profound insights (gnosis) into spiritual thinking. Alchemy is therefore the science of spiritual thinking and how to bring it to fruition. It is an initiatory process that has its antecedents in antiquity but that is now coming of age in your present biosphere. I will bring this subject new life in my next incarnation.

13 Joining the Dots

An aspect of Metaphorical Psychology is the use of language to reveal actual inner processes that bring about positive changes in consciousness. Alchemical language is rich in such symbolism. For instance, the classical alchemical process of boiling out dross in the cauldron, leaving only gold, is explaining a general feature of how consciousness can undergo transmutation and transformation. It begs a number of questions. What is the cauldron? What is the dross? What is the process of boiling or heating? What is the gold?

Then there is the more complex alchemical language describing various stages in the transmutational process. So the boiling must pass through three primal stages, represented by salt, sulphur and mercury. Increasingly complex alchemical formulas use astrological and hermetic symbols. But to simplify this vast and complex occult topic I only want to keep to the main branches. The cauldron is the vessel in which the operations take place. It is at the heart of the laboratory. If the laboratory itself is your physical body, the cauldron is your psyche or soul. The actual boiling or heating process describes various stages in inner shifts of consciousness. These changes are not arbitrary but rather controlled in ways that allow for safety and eventual success of the experiment. The dross is everything within the psyche of an inferior quality; everything that is not the best quality. Therefore, by contrast, gold is the best.

The aim of alchemy is simply one of achieving enlightenment or full potential. Alchemy is therefore a symbolic language parallel to Tantric and Yogic language. Spiritual psychology also shares many of these elements. They all have a common aim of being systems of generalised principles to help the true spiritual seeker obtain the goal of transformation and transmutation of consciousness and body.

Paracelsus brought alchemical symbolism into sophisticated levels of depth psychology long before psychology becamea commonly recognised branch of knowledge. He was an initiate of wisdom schools by incarnational hereditary and sought to alchemically transform his own consciousness and use of language to evolve the European psyche into future streams of integrative growth. This he continued to do in following incarnations, and as such he belongs to a soul cluster that is working globally in many related fields, that in your world tend to appear separate, but are not so.

Joining dots is a way of discovering connections that exist below the level of surface nomenclature. A potent orientation engendered in your time of scientism and industrialisation was 'specialisation'. Specialisation separated many related areas of life-study into increasing numbers of sub-branches until the branches appeared essentially unrelated. This outer process of separation became an inner splitting apart within the psyche itself. Alchemy in this context belongs to those psychological and metaphysical processes of re-joining dots that in reality were never separate.

The implications for the individual psyche and human societies are immense. Metaphoric psychology will empower language by reinstating words that have visual potency. Such language will not be dry and abstract but will penetrate into deeper levels of innate soul qualities and a recognition or re-awakening can then occur. In the process many illusions can be burnt away.

Those who work together alchemically share a type of common laboratory and the cauldron itself becomes a type of communal psychic vessel. Let these words inspire you.

Part 4

MANIFESTATION

Bringing soul gifts from invisible spaces

14 Shadows & Language

In your psychological linguistic parlance the word 'shadow' has more recently been employed as metaphor for the weaker and less desirable aspects of the human condition. In this I too had a part to play in my previous incarnation. Jung also brought this word into common usage. This meaning of shadow can be likened with the alchemical term, dross. As such, connections between the meanings of words are related to the intentions behind the words, what they are pointing towards.

Metaphorical psychology is motivated by a sincere desire to uncover the deepest meaning that words convey. Behind its outer appearance language has differing motivations and experiential levels. Humans generally don't give much thought to this. For example, one motivation behind words is purely practical: "Would you please pass the spoon.". Wanting to make a statement of fact motivates another quite different use of words: "This is a spoon."

Then there are levels of language that are more deeply motivated, and you tend towards describing these as scientific, psychological, philosophical or spiritual: "What is that tree?, What is the nature of consciousness?, What is a metaphor?, Does God exist?"

Language is, therefore, a mighty, complex labyrinth that colors understanding and perception to a great degree. It must be said that language has been, from the very outset, both a force for unification and division, leading towards clarity and confusion, facilitiating war and peace.

In its potential depths, language can be employed in transforming consciousness and human society. Metaphorical psychology is not a way of restricting language in yet another system, it is rather a way of realizing that all language has a metaphorical quality, because words point to things beyond themselves.

Metaphors are more than just metaphors! Language has a deeper mystical element. "Me and my shadow" is just one example.

15 Expressing from Silence

How does an incarnated human avoid the many pitfalls of language? In deep, calm inner silence, one can experience a state of being without mental interpretation and general chatter. In that space thought and language can emerge from experiential silence. What type of language is it that can emerge from silence? In real silence there is a transcendence of ordinary mind. If one can allow silence to embrace consciousness, identity and belief disappear. Consciousness itself becomes the alchemical gold. This is the paradoxical state of no-mind as Zen refers to it, except there is no it.

What quality of language can or should then emerge? In a place beyond knowledge, what do you know? The multi-dimensionality of consciousness can be recognised if one allows for the metaphor, 'All is consciousness.' There is a primal knowing within consciousness, but what exactly does one know? Infinite consciousness is an empty canvas. What will the artist express onto the canvas? What picture? In terms of the mind, what words are worthy of expression?

The threshold between silence and language invites a portal into unified dimensionality, a state where frictions are resolved into harmonies. And the greatest of these connected dimensions is that of silence and language whether couched in these words, or others metaphorically pointing to the same experiential truth. This is an aspect of hermeneutics whereby mind can look into its own depth and discover consciousness beyond any karmic conditioning.

Education would be doing your world a tremendous service if children were introduced to forms of simple emptiness meditation from an early age (five and onwards). This practice would be gradually cultivated and at around eight years of age expanded into various forms of meditative action, such as any physical movement that transcend ordinary mental activity, and then around puberty expand again into introduction to metaphorical psychology, as a way of exploring the power and uses of language. Children have natural metaphysical orientations until the rational indoctrination of culture swamps this and turns them into conforming atheists.

Of course I am generalizing but I am making a point. That is how metaphors operate. They make points. They invite resonances. They suggest ways to explore beyond social conditioning. They help to liberate a mind that is hooked to external group-think and cultural myopia. Creative debating, where even young children get to be heard in a safe environment and learn to listen to others, is most important. I'll end this session with another common metaphor: it's never too late to learn new tricks.

16 Form & Creativity

The topic of 'standardization' deserves an airing. But first a lead-in.

There are two potentially complementary forces existing in your universe and biosphere, micro and macro-cosmically. These two forces have been described and understood in many differing ways, for instance, as yang and yin. What you need to comprehend is that there are two essential qualities involved and naming them with a high degree of accuracy is important. One force is 'formative' and the other 'creative'. By formative is meant also uninformative and this expresses as multi-dimensional modes of conformity to fixed laws and principles. The other force is creatively free to express spontaneously and without limitation. Either of these forces expressing and manifesting without a healthy balanced complementariness becomes unstable. Nature, both cosmological and earthly reveals obvious disturbances when such imbalances occur.

It is glaringly obvious that your planet is suffering from gross imbalance caused by human stupidity. This stupidity leans heavily towards domination by formative forces at the expense of creative forces. Creativity is largely either marginalized or narrowly used in the service of conformity. Therefore 'standardization' in this context is what happens when uniformity becomes the dominating power.

This imbalance is at the heart of your planetary and human crisis. It is fundamentally a psychic imbalance. When formative energies overwhelm creativity the entire manifestation becomes mechanical and lifeless. Souls lose their creative enthusiasm and life is felt to be meaningless except in evolutionarily regressive ways. Metaphorical language is replaced by cold, utilitarian, overly practical, scientifically conformist and standardized usages.

Creativity slowly dies and is even outlawed. The artist must then courageously do battle, and so must the creative souls in all areas of human endeavor. The use of language needs to be a significant part of a cultural revolution and renaissance that rebalances creativity with formulas and systems. The downflux of creative energies from trans-dimensional sources must also be a part of this shift.

The history of the gradual overwhelming domination of standardization over creativity belongs to the exponential growth of industrialization and technology, together with materialistically driven economics and centralized power. The use of language as a tool in this process, through media, educational and advertising channels is especially dominant. Like any seesaw though, the tilt must eventually rebalance if a total betrayal of humanity is to be avoided.

17 A Charmed Life

There is a secret that we discarnate souls are aware of that I am going to try and let you in on. It is possible for incarnated souls to lead 'charmed lives', but this is not as linear or simple as it might sound.

Those who are linked to soul clusters doing important missionary work have access to help beyond what is apparent. The principle of freedom means that we cannot intervene without your permission or request, and even then the nature of any inter-dimensional dynamic follows directions that cannot be dictated to by limited incarnated perspectives. Hence, the 'charmed life' referred to can be both less and more beyond what is expected or desired.

From a more expansive discarnate view, the influences flowing like rain-showers into incarnate circumstances are a part of expansive evolutional processes. When the more spiritually sensitive incarnated souls are attuned and aware of the special synchronicity and grace that arranges circumstances in ways that further the greater evolutional missions, waves of gratitude and peace can sweep through mind and heart. Then one can say 'I am living a charmed life.'

The way to start living a charmed life is to align thought and feeling to one's greater mission. This is the key. It implies a dedication towards a transformational process. This possibility is your destiny, so why waste time and energy on lesser useless divergences? Related to this topic is the correct understanding of the 'Law of Attraction,' and also a contemporary insight into 'initiation.'

Part 5

TRANSFORMATION

Birthing anew, from death's released grip

18 Initiation

The meanings ascribed to initiation across culture and time are so numerous that the topic almost becomes swamped in obscurity. Traditionally initiations were serious moments of ritual shrouded in secrecy. They were meant to signify the experiential crossing of mystical thresholds. Secrecy was meant to protect sacred knowledge from the profane and unprepared. These types of initiatory processes still occur, but they are joined in your present world by many other less austere forms of initiation. The understanding of 'initiation' has mostly fallen into confused obscurity. The depth of meaning that it once had has been all but lost. In your present world it is more like a badge or ego decoration, and this leaves the question, 'What is spiritual initiation really?'

Fourth-dimensional consciousness only knows its own mental concepts. There is no recognition of a deeper stratum of consciousness. At this level of consciousness, initiation cannot mean anything other than another concept. In other words it doesn't really mean anything. For initiation to really begin to mean something it must include fifth-dimensional consciousness, and it is here that your modern earthly understanding becomes full of opportunities, but also great dangers. Old initiation processes were developed to be as safe as possible for the initiate or neophyte. Truly wise adepts guided mystery schools, and true mastery was generally achieved only after long years of inner study and experience.

Your world has dramatically changed, and few have the time or energy for such serious transformational processes. Souls have also evolved to a degree that qualities arising from initiation are embedded and await reawakening, rather than long arduous processes, unless a soul chooses a monastic life. For most this is not a viable option or desire. Therefore, forms of initiation have undergone massive change.

Where initiations are not fourth-dimensionally superficial and hence have true power, many can take advantage. But this has allowed for multiple complicated traps and invitations to non-integrated states of disturbance, some quite acute. Psychiatry has attempted to address this problem by believing that so-called 'chemical imbalances' can be treated pharmaceutically. For many incarnations I said that such mental and emotional disturbances are actually sicknesses of the soul, or spiritual disturbances that can be addressed by spiritual methods. In other words, forms of safe initiation.

19 Integrative Psychology

Keith has unknowingly worked together with me on understanding the various dynamics of soul disintegration. He used a term, 'vertical dissonance'. It is heading in the right direction.

I realise that a soul who is intimately karmically linked is struggling at this time, and seeks any authentic help that can flow through into fourth-dimensional consciousness. That help is omnipresently available.

Firstly, I need to convey that disturbances are rarely isolated. They are complex examples of relationship dynamics. We are all involved and trigger and catalyze each other. This happens discarnationally too, but augmented in earthly space-time it expresses as physical gesture and tonal projections.

There are two major orientations of integrative psychology, that can be termed horizontal and vertical. We are simplifying this by our use of language, but this is necessary if you are to grasp important elements of this extremely complex topic. By horizontal integrative psychology or fourth-dimensional psychology is meant ways of interpreting experience within cultural and linguistic norms. In itself this is important but falls way short of being able to understand or integrate trans-dimensional experience. By contrast, vertical integrative psychology focuses on trans-dimensional experience and its integration into fourth-dimensional thought, speech and activity.

If atheists in their general conceptual beliefs discard any validity to fifth-dimensional or spiritual experience they are bound to interpret vertical dissonance only in fourth-dimensional terms. This was partly the cause of friction and the parting of ways between Freud and Jung. Horizontal psychology can only delve so far into what psyche or soul is. It has developed into a brain-centered approach that does not perceive the psyche as something other than combinations of electrical chemicals, biological and metabolic processes.

Integrative psychology must employ both horizontal and vertical processes in conjunction with each other, for soul healing to be successful. For this to happen it is vital that fifth-dimensional maturity is consistent and capable of employing fourth-dimensional space-time methodology and language. At the very base of any such integrated approach must be an acceptance and awareness of the reality of spiritual dimensions. This acceptance should not be confused with spiritual ideas or particular experiences, as it needs to be simply an essential experiential recognition of spirit, whether named as 'spirit' or as something 'bigger than thought and bigger than me.' Two souls who both recognise and accept spirit as reality can immediately feel at ease and feel they have a foundation from which to communicate. Vertical dissonance is then not viewed fourth-dimensionally as a chemical imbalance or psychosis in a narrow clinical sense, but rather as a disturbance between fourth and fifth dimensionality, and therefore at least the diagnosis is essentially clear even if the treatment is challenging and uncertain. This can offer hope, but unless a therapist or guide has been 'initiated' in a real sense, there can be interwoven dissonances between both and this can be understood as a relationship dissonance.

Can you see how variably complex this is? What do we actually bring to any relationship exchange? Hopefully the texts that are being translated from the discarnate realms, and the biographies being crafted, can join the avalanche of such creative endeavors that are sweeping into your global cultures.

20 Miracles

Miracles do happen! You are one! Miracles are only perceived as such fourth-dimensionally, and yet it is not inappropriate to use this word to describe a phenomenon that belongs to the category of fifth-fourth dimensional interplay. This interplay does not violate the principle of freedom.

Fifth-dimensional consciousness is not 'individuated' as fourth is. Both light and dark spiritual forces can interweave into fourth-dimensional manifestations. Spiritual forces are clustered and do not function like individuated human ego-minds do. Therefore there is a dark side to miracles too.

Synchronicities are miracles in that they are, as Jung referred to 'a-causal' phenomena. In other words, they defy normal space-time laws. In your realm the tendency is to notice positive synchronicities, those that are perceived as miracles, small and large. The negative synchronicities tend to be avoided and unnoticed, or they are referred to as unfortunate catastrophes. What is especially significant to be aware of is that both types of synchronicities or miracles are inter-dimensional interplays. Human beings have a say in how these interplays occur, but not a control. They are manifestations that obey fifth-dimensional laws, and cannot be controlled by fourth dimensional mentality or desire, only influenced. It is the influences that are important to acknowledge, even if their workings are out of one's control to direct. This is the real meaning of faith: knowing we influence the interplay of inter-dimensional forces without having fourth-dimensional control. It is not blind faith.

The awakening soul perceives in miracles the meaningful 'hand of God.' Within synchronistic events there is a sense of karmic justice that transcends limited human viewpoints, and belongs rather to a natural law of universal balance. When consciousness realizes this law as it plays through a particular individual soul-life, there is a deep acceptance of existence as it is. This is the gateway to peace and responsibility. Miracles have a secret message for those who can read the script of life with spiritual eyes.

21   Destiny, Freedom & Love

The ultimate destiny of a soul is to be free to be. To be what? To be free 'to be free'. What does this mean? It means that a soul cannot ever be robbed of its inherent freedom. This is a secret power and inner truth that must be reconciled with any system or structure manifesting in fourth-dimensional existence. It is a part of destiny that will not be denied.

Source freely chose to create our universe and planted the seed of freedom into the creation. Deep within every soul there is the desire to experience freedom. Indeed, this quality underpins everything we do and are. Destiny therefore has, as its primary impulse, a desire to be free.

When a soul freely chooses to do something it has an element of destiny related to that action. But there is a caveat. Destiny in its greatest evolutional context requires freedom to be aligned with sacred purpose. When a soul is not aligned with sacred purpose the desire for freedom is not a part of ultimate destiny. Sacred purpose is another way of describing universal and unconditional love: Love of the Creator for creation.

When pure love is returned from creature to Creator, destiny has reached its zenith. This love must be freely experienced and shared. Love in this context is a full experience of sacred union. It is the merging of destiny, freedom and love in an omnipresent and omnipotent experience that both transforms and transcends energy into a totally integrated universe. Uni-verse meaning 'one poem' symbolically.

Metaphors abound in your world mythological literature that point to this ultimate destiny. It is Uroborus where mouth meets tail in a mystical circle. It is divine metamorphosis. It is sacred love underlying all lesser forms of love. It is your destiny!

Part 6

METAMORPHOSIS

Be at peace with struggle

22 Beyond Suffering

The genesis of the malignancy that afflicts humanity is the desire for sensory experience. This desire becomes a force that splits off from the universe and regards itself as rightfully separate. When consciousness becomes trapped in personal desire at the expense of the greater welfare of living beings, suffering begins. Suffering is a state of separation and elitism. There is no real love in elitism. Sensory desire is therefore a weak substitute for love.

This malignant egotism has infiltrated every inner and outer facet of your earthly realm. But beneath the surface of this cesspool of suffering is the pure impulse for freedom, and within that a sacred purpose. There can be no greater overcoming than that of reconciling freedom with sacred purpose and love.

A turnabout can only begin to happen if consciousness recognizes its own separatist tendencies and resolves to transform them. Illusions that are consequences of separatist thinking must be seen for what they are. It may appear that a collective coma has created a hell on earth, but it wouldn't take a lot for there to be a mass awakening, despite all appearances. It is for this reason that there are forces at play that will desperately attempt to thwart any move towards mass awakening. This cannot succeed, but only delay.

Many present incarnated souls that have been silenced in past incarnations are working towards a mass awakening, and let it be known, so are we who are part of your soul cluster. Do not despair, despite the great trap. Let me help you understand, and begin to morph into fifth-dimensional stability.

Materialism has become so overwhelmingly rife in your world that sensitive souls who yearn for spirit can feel suffocated. Souls have sought to escape from the consequences of human obsession with sensory experience that they themselves have brought into being. There is no escape. When a soul stops trying to escape and simultaneously stops seeking gratification from the endless search for sensory experience, a collapse back into this moment 'now' can occur. There is nothing to do and nowhere to go. The universe is doing and going.

You are infected by existential desire for experience. That is the meaning of the wise saying, 'Be in the world, not of it.' The truth is, you are in it. You cannot escape being in 'a' world, whether this or another, whether physical or metaphysical. The pure state of being is omnipresent. Within this pure state there is nowhere to go and nothing to do, therefore whatever you do and wherever you go, in reality you are unconsciously in the pure state. This is transcendental consciousness. Paradoxically, you are then doing and not doing. In the pure state, the question, 'What should I do?' takes on an entirely different perspective. When fourth-dimensional doing and going becomes meaningless, you can collapse into deeper being. The needs that belong to the infected soul, and that seek to impossibly fulfill a longing that cannot be fulfilled, can be perceived for what they are.

A soul can see this realm of 'hungry ghosts' everywhere about, reflecting one's own insatiable desire. And yet, if your eyes are opening, a sublime shift can begin. From within great turbulence, there is found peace. From within meaningless doing and going, there is found acceptance and stillness. A soul can then apply whatever has been absorbed from meditation. Theory can become a living practice. No one can take this inner journey for someone else.

Beyond space-time, I can project energy to another as a form of inter-personal and inter-dimensional communication, but I cannot force or coerce. I can give freely and accept that others can receive freely or choose freely to reject what I give. In this way our karma and destinies are formed. I can take on some emotional karma that belongs to another, but then I must release it for both of us. If we realize we are helpers in this collective drama, then it behoves us to strengthen our inner constitutions: for it is not for ourselves alone that we live.

23 Through the Trapdoor

There is a trap but also a trapdoor. The way through the trapdoor is also a great risk. It can be no other way. Souls bring their baggage with them to the threshold. Every buried past escapism comes to meet and tempt us. There is no way to avoid facing the shadow of one's past. This is a disguised blessing, because eventually it will be the great overcoming. Resistance will collapse or be surrendered. Your entire multi-dimensional self will then alchemically transform.

Many earthbound souls are now in processes of awakening, but in their conflicted partial states try to help others and create both clarity and confusion. Souls who are truly transformed and are worthy to be regarded as great teachers of humanity are few and far between, and generally do not offer their services in the marketplace of naïve, struggling humanity. Nonetheless, the miasmic interweaving of partially awakened souls is a part of the greater evolutionary process. Eventually souls will improve their capacity to discern, dedicate and focus. Again you cannot do this for another. You can truly bring a willing horse to water, but you can never make it drink.

Some souls, that are powerfully karmically-connected, play out especially intense and intimate entanglements. This capacity for intense entanglement will eventually be coupled with wise discernment and will lead to relationships that truly lead through the trapdoor and into the light of stable consciousness. Nothing is totally wasted. The big picture is really very, very, big. Stay connected!

24 Sorrow

There is a deep river of sorrow that is far deeper than personal sorrow. This is experienced as sadness that has no causal link alone, even if particular events trigger it. When a soul accepts this deep sorrow and doesn't try to escape or soften its sharp edges, nor confuses it with personal sadness, which is only the shallow aspect, then a shift in energy can occur.

This deep sorrow is one's connection with humanity, and it includes those with who one has especially powerful karmic ties, because they are not separate, and in reality are microcosmic relationships that mirror one's connection to all souls. This deep sadness needs to be fully felt and accepted. It is the escape from feeling this by many means that creates various levels of trapped suffering. The key capacity here is to be able to fully feel this sorrow without reaction. In other words, bear it.

It is a the way through the trapdoor. I feel so sad for human and non-human suffering. So sad for the self- created ignorance that holds suffering in place. So sad for a humanity lost in materialism. So sad for all the animals and nature so abused and unloved. And so sad for the personal encounters that are examples of suffering and lost-ness. This river of sorrow is my loving connection to life and inspiration to serve and help. You are beginning to accept and understand this sadness. It is shared by all who are awakening.

25 An Amoral Principle

The law of attraction is so that you consciously and unconsciously attract the entire spectrum of what you then refer to as 'my life.' The attributes within consciousness are as tentacles that move from within to form attachments externally.

For example, if I have an inner attribute of need for control, this will seek out externally those I can control. If others have an inner attribute of desiring to be controlled and the two meet, a dynamic may occur driven by the law of attraction.

Another example could be those who seek a genuine meditative path being attracted to the same teacher and ashram. There could be a common type of attribute and each person can experience something bigger than their own desire. Therefore the inner qualities you cultivate the most will attract similar energies and manifestations. If an inner attribute is one of naivety, experiences may be attracted that mirror one's lack of insight and realization. Those whose inner attribute is to prey on and exploit the naïve may be especially attracted to those who can be used in that way. This is the 'amoral' law of attraction. It is how growth can happen. It is how even animals learn.

There is an ever-changing flux of energies exchanging, attracting and repulsing. Within this flux you can consciously develop those attributes that you recognize as the most worthy of empowering. As you do this you are shaping your destiny along particular pathways. Everything then obeys a cosmic law of consequences.

In my previous incarnation I tried to impart my insights into personal psychological and spiritual transformation by way of empathy and metaphorical story-telling. Art too played a part, but what underpinned these interpersonal processes was a fundamental insight into what constituted deep alchemical change. I understood at a profound depth that I, as with everyone else, was the architect of my life. This insight was so potent that it guided my work for most of my earthly years.

I realized that those who came to me for help were in the exact same situation as me, except for one detail. That detail provided the impetus for my life's work. If you know through and through that you attract those elements to you that you experience as your life, you can take full responsibility for your existence and your destiny.

If you overcome those inner attributes accumulated over many incarnations that thwart your optimal potential you are on the way to redirecting your destiny in ways that are as a tree being replanted in good soil and later bearing good fruit as a consequence. No malignant force can coerce or control you without your conscious or unconscious agreement.

Part 7

AWAKENING

Do not spurn utopian visions!

26 Inner Revolution

There are so many cross-waves of influence in your present global societies. The proliferation of electronic media with its almost infinite miasma of information and opinions creates for many a confusing situation. What does one believe? Who does one trust?

This is where a portal into deep inner space is required. What does one find in this inner sanctum? A space where no information or opinion exists. Here, consciousness must surrender control and trust in a greater reality. For incarnated souls this threshold is experienced differently from where I am. You experience this physically too. The threshold includes a physiological dimension for you, and this must be endured. Alchemy is therefore an embodied phenomenon.

This is why yogic and meditative exercises are so important. I inherited knowledge of yoga and meditation that could be transferred into a western psychic constitution. These practices others can do too. The way to transfer eastern practices into a western psyche is of great significance to your western societies now.

Massive amounts of energy have been poured into the materialistic global empire. Almost all of your earth's resources and populations have become enslaved in a global corporate, technological, militaristic, political mechanism that threatens not only your planet but also the sacred essence of humanity.

Only an inner revolution can begin to turn this around and bring the great advances in technology under the guidance of spiritual consciousness. Such a revolution must come about from mass inner changes. There is one form of mass popular communication that could play a leading role in this, and that is global media.

27 Consciousness

I have shared an approach to understanding consciousness with my biographer in his dreams. Indeed inter-dimensionality within dreaming is another topic to delve into at a later time.

But now 'consciousness' is the topic. What is consciousness essentially? What does it mean for consciousness to be aware of itself? Consciousness sits behind all thought. This insight if experienced deeply can be the portal into a major shift in consciousness itself and can have positive revolutionary consequences for life, both personally and beyond.

The time is ripe in your earthly realm to exchange the metaphor of 'God' to that of 'Consciousness.' It is time to drop from the periphery into the center: from external to innermost: from thought to thinker.

Consciousness is the universal backdrop to your universe and your individuality. This must become a deep self-evident insight and not merely a passing interesting concept. Consciousness needs to rest in itself. This is the real significance of meditation. From within this essential awareness, questions can be asked with clarity, impossible for other types of consciousness. Every aspect of your individuality is an outgrowth from Consciousness through space-time.

As this is an ongoing process you can change its nature, content and direction at any moment. Pivotal in this is awareness of the essential nature of consciousness, as a-priori experience In other words, when consciousness becomes self-aware. The proof of the pudding is in the eating!

28 Know Thyself!

Your divine mission is to know who you are. When you know who you are, you will know who I am. This does not imply sameness of individuality, quite the contrary. It implies that behind our unique individualities is one universal reality. This supreme reality is both greater than you, and who you really are. You are the individuated manifestation of who you really are, as a universal Supreme Being. You are Consciousness with its natural supreme attributes. To know these attributes, know yourself as universal unified Consciousness.:Know thyself!

You are yourself, so know who you are. You share in all manifestations, so to know who everyone is, know 'you'. To know the essential nature of everything, know the nature of consciousness. This is the medicine for your world's ailments. Wise teachers would help children remember who they are. This wisdom should never have been forgotten. The individuated soul who forgot, gave birth to forgetfulness, and we are the descendants. But we also have a divine mission to remember and help others do likewise. There is no greater mission and service than this. This is your destiny: to remember who you are and to help others awaken too. The outgrowth of individuality can then be understood as service via the natural creative gifts developed and developing through space-time. My personal biography is simply concerned with that, as are other biographies. This is every soul's highest evolutional mission.

Animals and nature help in this universal mission in ways peculiar to their individual capacities. As a human incarnation you have vast potential if first you know who you are. You are Consciousness prior to all manifestation and the outgrowth from Consciousness that can be expressions of primary qualities embedded in Consciousness itself. You are One and many. You are a unique individual but for this to not become a secondary source of egoistic pride and separate elitism, you must remember the great Source that everyone and everything is.

Without remembering who you really are, words such as love, truth, humility, wisdom, intelligence and trust have little meaning. Without knowing who you are experientially, philosophy, theology and psychology have only shallow significance. There is no deep soul healing without knowing thyself.

29 Wakefulness & Sleep

Human consciousness can be as lost in sleep as in wakefuleness. Conversely, sleep can be a source of insight, creativity and purposeful processing, as can be the wakeful state. More to the point, the two states of sleep and wakefuless flow into and influence each other. The distinction humans generally make between these two states is both false and a hindrance to the potential existing in the sleep state.

There is a tendency to think of dreams as unimportant and one-dimensional. This tendency has helped to diminish the powers inherent within consciousness. When you develop wakefully, this flows into increased capacities within sleep and vice versa.

There are many levels of sleep and dream, just as there are many levels of waking consciousness. These waking and sleeping levels of consciousness can generally be understood as closer or further from universal intelligence and power. As Elucia described at length, souls evolve through many expanding levels of manifestation, from most subtle to most energy-dense.

Where I exist now there is no sleep, only rest. Sleep belongs to the physical state of existence. Sleep for humans is also rest, but also much more. Without physical experience the soul can be closer to where I am, that is, interdimensional. Interdimensionality can be cultivated both within sleep and by way of wakeful meditative practices and deep consciousness exploration. Any incarnated soul who has cultivated deep consciousness work should be aware of various levels of dreaming. At the most superficial level of dreaming, dream symbolism reflects physiological experience, including digestive processes. This is why eating soon before sleeping is not good from a psychological and spiritual perspective.

In your present world environment, technological influences can affect dreaming too. Such dreams are generally without clarity and depth. But when an incarnated soul does good inner work, including healthy living practices, dreaming can enter into levels that are less superficially symbolic and more metaphorical. Such dreams can be prophetic, instructional, intuitive, guiding, healing, revelatory and generally meaningful, given that there is some degree of waking memory and follow up process.

Then at an even deeper level, symbolic dreaming ceases and a type of direct communication ensues that closely approximates the ways that discarnate souls relate and experience each other. It is at this deep level that interdimensional communication and energy sharing occurs. This deep level of interdimensionality can happen during human wakefulness too, and I would like to reiterate, both deep inner work during human wakefulness and sleep enhances each other.

Beyond these deep levels of experience, there is the deepest of all: that is beyond all energy, and is known as deep sleep or dreamless sleep, and in wakefulness as samadhi, meditation, or emptiness. This is the Sabbath of discarnate and incarnate experience, the time of total rest. Hopefully this explanation will inspire you to pay more attention to dreams and in general, cultivate deeper modes of inner experience, insight and purpose.

30 A Final Blessing

Elucia, yourself and others who are a part of our soul cluster and extended inter-cluster can communicate interdimensionally with each other. But the time has come to bring this part of the work to a natural close.

We here are pleased to sanction this example of interdimensional collaboration. To now craft this into a book is the challenge ahead. Then to do what is possible to bring it to receptive incarnated souls. We shall hopefully pick this up too during our next incarnations.

This has been an experiment in interdimensional communication and collaboration, not the first of its kind, nor will it be the last. Across your planet there is a proliferation of similar experiments, in what Elucia has described as transitioning from fourth to fifth-dimensional consciousness. It has been known in Christian culture as the second coming of Christ. Whatever cultural or religious cloak you place over this transition, the essential change is within consciousness itself. Our intention and hope is that within your busy incarnated lives that includes other important work besides this, you nevertheless craft this into a book that will reach many, and contribute to the very shift so desperately needed in your earthly biosphere and mass consciousness.

We shall continue to guide you from our stellar realms as long as we are discarnate, and cooperate in mysterious formations as we cross over between our incarnate, discarnate and transcarnate existences. It is for you who are incarnated to bring this model of collaboration into your earthly fields of work. You have been doing this work consciously and subconsciously for most of your adult lives. Therefore you also naturally recognise this soul quality in others. You too are recognised by others. We too guide them. We are all part of a mission so beautiful and full of grace that you would weep with joy if you but glimpsed its magnificence.

We here dedicate this endeavour to the betterment of your earthly evolution, now, and as it develops towards an awakening of the sacred mission for which we all intimately exist.

Blessings!

Postscript

It is clear now, at this time of writing in 2021, that the global cabal, the small number of incarnated humans that hold the reins of power, are initiating processes of change that are radical and irreversible. This represents a quantum shift in civilisation; a new evolutional epoch. The problem is that it is being engineered largely by stealth and deceipt.

Only a transformed consciousness can bring about a New World Order that is worthy of the true human potential. That is why Parelsitus, in transmitting his 'thirty pieces of gold', is urging us to engage in an inner revolution. If thirty pieces of silver is a metaphor of the betrayal of true human potential, then thirty pieces of gold, is a metaphor indicating what we individually and collectively are capable of: no less than a total recalibration and transformation of our world, from inside-out. Humanity stands on a threshold that cannot be avoided. The 'Old World Order' that we are entrenched in within every area of human life must indeed transform, but into what? A so-called 'New World Order' that is governed by the old consciousness will create a more devastating nightmare than the one we have already co-created.

The good news is that souls such as Parelsitus have dedicated missions to awaken humanity to the possibility of a truly transformed future. A 'new world order' that is an authentic expression of honesty, freedom, creativity, kindness, compassion and love.

The potential to awaken awaits.

It is urgent that it happens.

Thirty pieces of gold will help.

(From Savitri, Book III, Canto IV)

I saw the Omnipotent's flaming pioneers
Over the heavenly verge which turns towards life
Come crowding down the amber stairs of birth;
Forerunners of a divine multitude,
Out of the paths of the morning star they came
Into the little room of mortal life.

I saw them cross the twilight of an age,
The sun-eyed children of a marvellous dawn,
The great creators with wide brows of calm,
The massive barrier-breakers of the world
And wrestlers with destiny in her lists of will,
The labourers in the quarries of the gods,
The messengers of the Incommunicable,
The architects of immortality.

Into the fallen human sphere they came,
Faces that wore the Immortal's glory still,
Voices that communed still with the thoughts of God,
Bodies made beautiful by the spirit's light,

Carrying the magic word, the mystic fire,
Carrying the Dionysian cup of joy,
Approaching eyes of a diviner man,
Lips chanting an unknown anthem of the soul,
Feet echoing in the corridors of Time.

High priests of wisdom, sweetness, might and bliss,
Discoverers of beauty's sunlit ways
And swimmers of Love's laughing fiery floods
And dancers within rapture's golden doors,
Their tread one day shall change the suffering earth
And justify the light on Nature's face.

- Sri Aurobindo

OTHER BOOKS BY KEITH SIMONS

Quest: A Mystical Autobigraphy
Portal: Awakening to Being
Biography of a Russian Yogi
Elicia: A Multidimensional Biography
Poetica Esoterica
Resons for Being: From Free Diving to Transformation

Forthcoming Books:
Merged Voices
Struggles and Aspirations
Age of the Consciosness Soul

Contact:
Keith Simons
globalquest28@gmail.com
+613 0499 272 820
www.spiritual-narratives.net

9 780975 836538